Herbs for Northern Gardeners

Dave Sands

LONE PINE

Homeworld

The Publisher:
Lone Pine Publishing
#206, 10426-81 Avenue
Edmonton, Alberta, Canada
T6E 1X5

Canadian Cataloguing in Publication Data
Sands, Dave.
    Herbs for northern gardeners

    (Homeworld)
    ISBN 0-919433-99-5

    1. Herbs. 2. Herb gardening. I. Title.
II. Series.
SB351.H5S35 1992   635'.7   C92-091196-X

Original Compilation: Keith Ashwell
Editorial: Phillip R. Kennedy, Roman Kravec
Homeworld Editor: Lloyd Dick
Cover Illustration: Linda Dunn
Printing: Friesen Printers. Altona, Manitoba, Canada

The publisher gratefully acknowledges the assistance of the Federal Department of Communications, Alberta Culture and Multiculturalism and the Alberta Foundation for the Arts in the production of this book

Contents

A Plant for All Seasonings

A herb is any plant of which the shoots and leaves die back at the end of each growing season. Thus it can be an annual, biennial or perennial, and many kinds of plant are described as 'herbaceous'.

Most gardeners refer to herbs as those plants whose leaves or stalks, seeds or flowers, or all four, have food, flavouring, aromatic or medical uses to humankind.

Herbs can be sweet-smelling. They can be pungent. They can bring a colourful flavour to a dish. They can add a savoury overtone or undertone.

Herbs may identify themselves by aroma — the natural release of their essential oils. Or they may require bruising, pressing or boiling to release their colourful culinary qualities.

Today, as long ago, herbal aromas can be useful and comforting to us. If you are affected by the air around you, full of the smell of other people's cooking, traffic, industry or illness, simply cutting and washing a branch of any of the culinary (cooking) herbs in this book will fill your living space with a natural scent that will revive and placate. And then, those herbs will be there for use in your next meal. Try basil, rosemary, oregano or thyme.

Gathering Herbs

In the footsteps of our ancestors generations ago, we have re-discovered they joys of sachets of lavender tucked into our linen chests and potpourris left on a table or bookshelf to give our living rooms an air of freshness.

This book will help get you started in the wonderful world of herbs. The usefulness of these amazing plants is limited only by your imagination.

Herbs

Basil

Basil is an essential herb — it is easy to grow, prolific and easy to use. Seed or set out plants when ground is warm (May or June), provide good, rich soil in a sunny spot and keep the plant watered but not soaked. Plant a lot of basil, because you'll use a lot, and space it to about 30 cm (12 in.), after thinning. Pinch off the flower buds to encourage your basil to leaf out and harvest the young, tender leaves. Remember, its an annual outdoors, and its gone with the first frost of fall.

At least 45 varieties of basil exist. After you fall in love with it, look for *Ocimum citriodorum*, lemon basil, *O. crispum*, lettuce leaf basil, *O. minimum*, a small-leaved basil good for indoors, or *O. sanctum*, the holy basil of Hindu India.

Growing Basil
- Seed or transplant after last frost.
- Space 15 cm (10 inches), in good soil and sun, then thin to 30 cm after growth is established.
- Water well, keep soil moist.

Using Basil
Mince basil leaves and use in sauces (pesto), salads, with tomatoes, green vegetables, eggs and pastas.

Basil is a good house plant, and can be a full-time kitchen companion if given a sunny window, daily misting and the necessary pinching-off. Grow it in good, sterilized potting soil indoors, starting it in the flats under glass or a greenhouse dome. Basil roots easily from cuttings in plain water.

Use basil fresh, and often, in summer. Basil leaves can be prepared in a blender, a steamer or they can be minced, torn, or eaten like lettuce in a tomato sandwich. Basil and garlic are like salt and pepper — use them together.

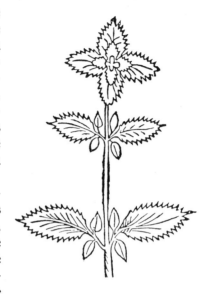

Basil

Basil has a lot of admirers, and many virtues. Gardeners say bees love basil — it has a marvellous clove-like scent that fills the garden. It's also said that basil repels flies.

Use basil carefully if you're new to it. Remember that when dried, basil's taste changes and becomes curry-like. Don't leave it out as a garnish — it discolours.

Borage

Borage is a big (to 1 m/3.4 ft. tall, 30 cm/1 ft. wide) plant with large leaves, pink-turning-to-blue flowers that bees love and a cucumber taste. It's a sturdy plant, and will self-seed for years. Be forewarned, though — it may not come up where you want it to. You can plant borage in your garden's poorest soil and shadiest places and it will still grow. Give it good soil and lots of water and you'll get a large, showy plant that will provide lots of tender leaves for salads, flowers to float in drinks and stalks to peel and cook as greens.

Borage needs plenty of space, so plant your borage seeds 50 cm (20 in.) apart. It grows tall, and it will spread as much

Growing Borage
- Direct seed 1.25 cm (1/2 in.) deep. Cover and water.
- Doesn't transplant well.
- Tall, wide plant — allow space.
- Will spread widely unless controlled.

Using Borage
New leaves minced in salads, peeled stalks boiled as greens, flowers for teas, garnishes.

as you let it. Borage is also an impressive indoor herb if you transplant small shoots into a large pot. The star shaped flowers will bloom with lots of light and regular watering through the winter.

Use the smaller, tender new borage leaves like mint leaves in drinks or teas. Try the flowers in drinks or salads. Finely chopped (minced) borage leaves are a good addition to lettuce, cucumber and potato salads. Try mixing your own salad dressings to control the flavour. If you're new to using herbs, remember its always easy to add more if you like the effect but hard to reduce an excessive amount.

Borage blooms are a bright blue colour. You can float these flowers in white wines and non-alcoholic coolers to great effect. Legends suggest that you can brew a tea from borage leaves for courage — there's a lot of potassium in this herb.

Borage

Chamomile

Chamomile is the tea herb. It has been sipped before bedtime by everyone from princes to Peter Rabbit. Make sure you use *Chamaemelum nobile*, or *Matriciaria chamomilla* for best results. It's important to get one of these varieties, because chamomile (also spelled camomile) is also found as a lawn grass substitute, *C. Treneaugue*, and as scentless field chamomile, which isn't very useful. The lawn variety does not flower.

Chamomile

Chamomiles grow from 25-50 cm (10-20 in.) tall. Most re-seed themselves year after year. Chamomile has no cooking uses but it does make a good skin care lotion and a soothing addition to bath water.

Plant chamomile in good soil in bright sun, and be prepared to control its growth by thinning or cutting back. Bunches can be divided to spread around or give away. When used as a ground cover, chamomile can be mowed, but it's not winter hardy.

Growing Chamomile
- Seed in spring in good soil in full sun.
- Spreads quickly: control by dividing, trim flowers to force thick growth.
- Low habit, pleasant odour, small flowers.

Using Chamomile
Herb tea and skin lotion, border planting, ground cover.

Chamomile's best use is in herbal tea. Because the flowers are small, picking enough for use can be tedious, so mix your own blend in the garden by carrying the tea pot with you. Take leaves from mints, lemon balm, rosemary and bergamot, and add chamomile blossoms. Fill loosely and brew like any other tea. Your taste will be your best guide. Pick on a sunny day, and dry chamomile flowers in a single layer on a fine, non-metallic screen. Store in a jar out of the light for a cup of heavenly herbal tea on a cold winter night.

Chervil

Chervil is a very accommodating herb. It's essential in French cooking, important in Italian cuisine and valuable in German, English and American menus. It helps gardeners because it grows well in shady spots and it grows quickly. In addition, it's not large, grows best from direct seeding, and if allowed to flower, produces a tiny but pretty white blossom.

Chervil is preferred over parsley in the French cooking techniques of *fines herbes* and *bouquet garni.* In fact, you can use chervil wherever you'd use parsley. Chervil leaves, chopped fine, can be used fresh in egg dishes (especially omelettes), in soups and in sauces for fish. Here's a great fish sauce idea: combine a teaspoon each of chervil and parsley and one crushed garlic clove. Squeeze a half lemon into the mixture and combine with two tablespoons of butter. Heat carefully and pour over fish just before serving.

Growing Chervil
- Grows well in shade, moisture, rich soil.
- Plant seeds after last frost.
- Use succession seeding for continuous crop.
- Cut flowers to maintain leaf growth.

Using Chervil
Leaves finely chopped, cut in butters, sauces, whole leaves in *fines herbes, bouquet garni.*

Plant chervil seeds in three week successions so you can always use new leaves. Chervil goes to flower quickly after leafing out, and continuous plantings can be more convenient than pinching out tiny buds. Since chervil grows well in the shade, it can fit in with taller plants in your vegetable garden, or mix in with tall perennial flowers. It will reach 45-60 cm (18-24 in.) in height, depending on conditions. Moist soil, light shade, and about 10 cm (4 in.) of space between plants are all essential for healthy chervil.

Freshness is important when you use chervil, so bringing it in from the garden when you need it is best. Despite all of these virtues, chervil can't be usefully preserved — it's a fair-weather friend. If you want year-round fresh chervil, try it as an indoor pot plant. You can start chervil from seed, as long as you keep the soil moist, but not soaking wet.

Chives

Chives are so easy to grow and use that many people don't know they're herbs. This member of the onion family is perennial nearly everywhere, and is a good indoor pot plant wherever you are. In milder areas, it's usually available most of the winter.

You can grow chives from a divided clump, from seed, or from nursery stock. They are good balcony plants because they're inexpensive and prolific in small spaces.

Chives need rich soil, sun and regular watering, with occasional manure or compost fertilizing. That means a good

---

Growing Chives
- Requires fertile, moist soil. Fertilize during growth.
- Useful as a border plant.
- Divide clumps to expand.

Using Chives
Chop stalks and use with eggs, salads, soups, *fines herbes*, cottage cheese, herb butter. Flowers can be used in salads.

site or good potting soil indoors. You can keep chives growing
by cutting with scissors at the base of the hollow, grass-like
stalk. Always leaving a few blades standing in the clump.

The flowers are a pretty pinkish-purple and should be cut
off after blooming. You can then divide the plant to create
more chive plants.

Chives are versatile plants with a delicate flavour. Use
them as a potherb (cooked in), in *fines herbes* mixes, salads,
herb butters, sour cream, egg dishes, tomato dishes, and of
course, you could sprinkle it on top of a baked potato.

Chives can be stored best by freezing.

Look for garlic chives (*Allium. tuberosum*), also called
oriental chives, for a milder-than-garlic flavouring.

Dill

Dill is universally known for
its connection with pickles.
It's more versatile than that,
however. Its leaves are great
with egg dishes, cheese, fish
and vegetables.

The seeds, flowers and
stalks can be used sepa-
rately or together, depending upon your pickling
recipe. Whole dill plants,
once they have gone to seed,
can be used to make dill
vinegar, (one plant per litre,
soaked for a week minimum,
then strained). Minced dill
leaves with lemon juice and
butter make a good spread

Dill

on warm bread, carrots or hot, steamed potatoes. Many fish
dishes call for a dill sauce.

Dill grows from seed and should be succession planted for
a continuous crop — the leaves should be used before the
plant flowers. Seeds appear after flowering and are ready for

---

Growing Dill
- Direct seed, thin, and stake.
- Needs sun, does well in acidic soil.
- Prepare soil deeply before seeding.

Using Dill
Seeds are essential in pickling. Leaves, usually minced, are great with fish, beans, beets, potatoes and in sauces.

---

use when they turn brown or beige. They usually shake off the plant, reseeding it for next year. A simple way to collect dill seed is to cut the plant off at the stem, tie bunches together and cover with a paper bag. Turn upside down and shake. More seeds will fall as the plant dries. The best way to preserve dill leaves by freezing — dried dill leaves don't retain much flavour.

Dill needs sun, and since it can grow to 60 cm (2 ft.), it should be placed behind shorter plants. Keep it away from fennel, but it can be companion planted with cabbage or cucumbers. Space it to 45 cm (18 in.) after seeds sprout and fertilize and water regularly. Dill will probably need staking when it gets tall.

Pickling recipes, fish dishes, vegetables and soups all use the flavour of dill. It's a basic, easy growing but delicate herb and should be added late in cooking, just before serving.

Fennel

There are three fennels to chose from. In a small garden, one of these large (1.25 m/5 ft.) plants may do. If you like fish, fennel will be a major cooking herb for you. If you like celery and Italian cooking, the Florence fennel variety (*azoricum*) is your choice. Bronze fennel, (*rubrum*) is equally useful and adds colour to your garden. But, the most popular fennel is *foeniculum vulgare*. You can seed it in spring and use it as a bedding plant. Fennel needs room and shouldn't be planted near dill or coriander.

Fennel is an old Mediterranean plant which was often used in ancient times as a laxative, an aid to digestion, an eyewash, a tea ingredient, as a vegetable and as a green in salads. Fennels belong in the same *Umbelliferae* family as parsley and dill.

Fennel

Fennel leaves — crumbled, chopped or whole — can be used raw and the stalks can be cooked with the fish. Barbecue fish, like salmon, with whole fennel leaves for a new taste.

Fennel leaves can be used throughout the season. Only harvest the top-growing, tender ones. Leaves can be mixed into cheese dishes or can be mixed with stalks and seeds to make tea.

Stalks *(of vulgare)* can be peeled or sliced and cooked quickly. Florence fennel is grown and used like celery — you may have seen it sold as finocchio. The bulb at ground level must be heaped up with soil (like potatoes) to blanch the root. Slice and cook or eat raw when the bulb is egg-sized. Fennel's flavour is stronger than celery's — anise or licorice are more apt comparisons.

Fennel seeds should be harvested when they're brown and ready to fall. Dry and store them away from moisture. These seeds are important in Italian cooking, especially sauces, salads and pasta dishes.

Growing Fennel
- Grows tall, needs sun, fertile but light soil.
- Plant seeds, thin to 30 cm (12 in.).
- Can tolerate dry soil. Doesn't transplant well.

Using Fennel
Leaves, whole or chopped, with fish dishes. Seeds with fish, chicken and pork recipes.

Garlic

Garlic is actually part of the onion family. However, it is mostly used like an herb — it's a seasoning, not an cooking ingredient. Garlic is the key to the flavour of any dish it's used in and an essential part of cooking in several cultures.

It's been said that if you know about garlic, there's nothing anyone can tell you about it, and if you don't, nobody can tell you what you're missing. If you don't regularly use garlic, why not give it a try?

Garlic is planted and grown like an onion — from seed garlic 'sets' or from the largest cloves from a previous crop. In cold climates, it can be planted early in spring with safety, and in mild zones it can be planted in October for spring harvest. It is a perennial in warmer climates.

Garlic needs good soil, sun and careful watering. Plant it the cloves vertically, 3.5 cm (1 3/8 in.) deep, 1.5 cm (1/2 in.) apart in each direction, and rotate the crop annually. Garlic is a good companion plant for roses, cabbage and gooseberries, because insects like aphids avoid it.

Since garlic is a member of the onion family, you may want to experiment with garlic chives (*Allium tuberosum*) or with ramsons (*A. ursinum*). Use the leaves of these two varieties as flavourings, for a milder garlic taste.

Growing Garlic
- Plant cloves (sets) early. Space widely.
- Needs sun. Can use poor soil, but thrives in good.
- Harvest when leaves turn yellow. Store in dry area.

Using Garlic
Essential in Mediterranean recipes, especially sauces (pesto), with chicken and lamb. Flavours butter, oils, dressings. You can't make a Caesar salad without it.

Lavender

Lavender is a colour, a cut flower, a fragrance, a ground cover, a bush, a hedge and much more. Lavender is the basis of the potpourri and sachet industry. This plant, associated with the English all over the world, got its start as a Mediterranean perennial, but its hardiness varies with variety. What doesn't vary is the visual attractiveness.

Colours range from white through pink to blue, and size ranges from the 20 cm (8 in.) dwarf munstead to the 1.2 m (4 ft.) hedge

Lavender

Lavandula spica. You'll find a wide range of sizes and colours in lavenders. You will succeed with these colourful herbs if you choose from nursery stocks which are hardy in your area. Lavender seeds need special care as they germinate.

Plant lavender with roses to protect them from lice. Choose a sandy, sunny, well-drained spot, and only add fertilizer in the fall. Add lime and prune in spring if you want bushy plants for hedging, or prune in fall after the flowers die

Growing Lavender
- Soil choice influences fragrance: sandy, dry, sunny spots are best.
- Add lime to soil for better flowers.
- Prune after flowering to control growth.
- Mulch in winter.

Using Lavender
Flowers are essential in pot pourris, sachets, and leaves and flowers for teas.

for a showy plant. Like any flowering plant, the fragrance is greatest just before buds are fully open. Cut the stalks for decorative uses and remove faded flowers on outdoor plants.

Lavender is versatile. Floral crafts, like potpourri and sachet making, require it extensively. Many grandmothers can tell about using lavender as a fragrance in their linen closets. It was also used in wash water and to flavour honey.

Three Lemon Herbs:
Balm, Basil and Verbena

North Americans associate the scent of lemon with cleanliness, summer and good times. Hence, lemon shows up in all sorts of products — dishwasher soap, car wax and deodorants. You can surround yourself with lemon, and enjoy it more, with these three herbs.

Lemon balm *(melissa officinalis)* produces leaves that will scent your hands and make a fine, hot, lemony tea. It will also add a distinctive flavour to sauces, salads, soups, lamb and chicken. Of the three lemon herbs, it's probably the most useful.

Lemon Balm

Lemon basil *(ocimum citriodorum)* is fragrant and as useful as any other basil. It's a small bush, about 60 cm (2 ft.) tall. It works great as a border plant because its fragrance is released when you brush by the leaves.

Lemon verbena *(Aloysi triphyllia)* can be grown as an outdoor or an indoor plant. Verbena is a large and diverse plant family and you may see it referred to as *Lippia citriodora*. Use its leaves in sachets, in teas, as a lemon rind substitute in cooking, and in flower arrangements.

Successful growing of these lemon varieties demands that you treat them as annuals. Start the seeds in flats and transplant after last frost in the spring, or use nursery stock. All three lemon herbs are commonly available. They all require good soil and full sun, and pruning back helps keep them decorative and under control. Self-seeding by lemon balm can create overcrowding problems in milder zones, so be sure to remove any new shoots to prevent overgrowth.

You can make lemon tea by picking five to eight fresh, new leaves and pouring boiling water over them, steeping the tea to taste. One teaspoon of minced leaves also makes great tea. Leaves picked before flowering starts are best for flavour. Try adding some leaves to your regular tea blend for a start. Iced lemon teas are a delicious summer treat.

Lovage

One lovage plant is enough for most cooks and gardeners. Although it's useful and pretty, it's also large and spreading. This herb is a member of the celery and carrot family and is a combination of useful leaves, stalks and roots. It's also considered a "strong" herb, so enjoy it with caution until you're used to it.

Lovage leaves are celery-like in shape and strong in flavour, and can be used in salads and greens. Lovage stalks, like celery, can be chopped or used whole, cooked or raw. The

---

Growing Lovage
- Transplant and allow plenty of space for growth, in deep moist soil.
- This slow growing, large plant, may need root division to maintain vigour.
- Can tolerate shade.

Using Lovage
Leaves, fresh or dried in salads, soups, stews. Stems like celery. Roots cooked in stews, etc.

roots, like carrots, are cooked into soups and stew. When lovage flowers, with a tiny but pretty yellow head in clusters (like dill), its seeds are useful additions to breads and stuffings. Many old family recipes use this versatile herb — lovage leaves and stalks were used for teas, infusions, and as cures fever or colic in herbal medicine.

Lovage is best grown from a nursery or garden centre plant because it's very slow from seed. It needs room and time. Space it 30 cm (1 ft.) from anything else when planting out. Make sure it is planted in deep moist soil with lots of organic matter, in direct sunlight. A spot against a fence might be chosen so lovage doesn't shade too much of the garden when it reaches its full height of up to 2 m (6 1/2 ft.). At best, it will take about three or four years to reach this height, and in many zones, the plant will die back and need a mulch to get through each winter. To grow more lovage, or to renew an old plant, dig up and divide the roots of a healty plant. Lovage can be a pot plant indoors and can be kept small if pruned back. Keep your lovage plant well fertilized and make sure the soil moist but not soggy.

Lovage can become one of the most useful herbs in your garden. Like many others, its value will grow with practice.

Sweet Marjoram

Sweet marjoram is a pleasant, low growing, useful herb that will fit in as a border plant or in a flower bed. It provides spicy, long-lived leaves that can be used either fresh or dried with eggs, soups, tomatoes, poultry and in stuffing and sausages.

Growing Marjoram
- Bedding plants or cuttings.
- Grows best in well-drained soil.
- Grows to 60 cm (2 ft.).

Using Marjoram
Leaves, fresh or dried, whole or crumbled in all but sweet foods, but especially with meats, tomatoes and fresh root vegetables. Use in small quantities.

It's a useful herb with all but sweet foods, having a distinct flavour with a tint of bitterness.

Sweet marjoram is an old herb, which may account for its variety of names. You may know it as pot marjoram, knotted marjoram, annual marjoram or garden marjoram. It was once called oregano, but this name is now generally used for the species *Origanum vulgare*. This herb is a tender perennial. In northern climates, it should be treated as an annual. It is best grown from bedding plants, because of its slow and uncertain

Marjoram

growth from seed. It can be expanded by taking cuttings and rooting them in summer, but it must be potted indoors to survive past the first frost in the fall.

Sweet marjoram grows well in full sun. Well drained, sandy, well-manured soil is important, and the plant should be pruned to help it grow bushy and compact. It has a pleasant silver-grey-green colour and tiny white flowers.

Sweet marjoram leaves are best used fresh, but they can be dried. Freezing doesn't preserve them well. This herb is versatile — use it with lamb, pork, beef and game meats, chicken, fish, broiled or baked shellfish, oyster and clam chowders. Vegetables such as carrots, cauliflower, peas, spinach, squash, mushrooms, broccoli and brussels sprouts can benefit from minced marjoram leaves sprinkled on during cooking. Stir this herb into pizza and spaghetti sauces, stuffings, egg dishes such as omelettes, potato salads and salad dressings, and use whole leaves in salads.

Sweet marjoram is a basic herb for potpourris and *bouquet garni*, and combines well with thyme, basil and parsley.

Mint

Mints come in a vast variety of sizes, shapes and smells. It can be confusing picking the right one, but since they're mostly grown from nursery stock, and sold in garden centres everywhere, there should be someone you can consult for a "culinary" or cooking variety. Spearmint *(Mentha spicata)* or peppermint *(M. piperita)* are the usual choices, but there are many other popular mint varieties. Many cuisines use unique mints — puleggio *(M. pulegium)* in Italian cooking, bowles or applemint *(M. sauveolens)* in English cooking and bergamot/orangemint *(M. Citrata)* in teas. Mints are often hybridized (crossed) to create attractive, new varieties. Some mints will only be available as nursery stock, not as seeds.

Mints are relatively easy to grow. They don't have special requirements for soil, moisture or light, and most will grow well in the shade.

One drawback of mints is that they tend to grow wildly if not controlled. You can control spreading by growing your mints in containers raised off the garden, in deep bottomless pots in the soil, or with steel or plastic dividers around them. These should be a minimum 30 cm (1 ft.) deep.

Mint rust disease can also be a problem. If you find rust — brown spots on the leaves — destroy the plants immediately and plant mint elsewhere next year, spacing them more widely.

Growing Mints
- Transplant bedding stock.
- Make sure roots cannot spread.
- Most varieties grow to about 60 cm (2 ft.).

Using Mints
Leaves, whole, crushed, chopped, in salads, with vegetables, in sauces, with meats, esp. Lamb, and as flavour in cooling drinks, or for hot or iced teas.

Different mints should not be planted together, or near chamomiles, but they are good companion plants for cabbages and tomatoes.

Mints can stand a far more alkaline soil than most herbs and can be grown easily from root cuttings. They transplant well.

Mints are perennials in all zones, but rotate their spot in your garden every two years — old growths of mints get coarse and lose flavour. Except for its invasive habits, it's an easy herb to work with.

The use of mints in the kitchen depends slightly on

Mint

your chosen variety. Normally, the leaves are harvested and used whole and crushed, chopped fine, or dried, crumbled and added during cooking. Mint and lamb are an essential combination, but mints are equally important with fresh vegetables, especially new potatoes, jellies and in summer coolers.

For a great cooler, float washed leaves on top of the mix. Any gin drink is a natural and the mint julep owes as much to mint as it does to bourbon.

Mint leaves of all varieties dry well and are often used in herb potpourris. Pick leaves after the morning dew has evaporated, and before the plant flowers, for maximum flavour. Dry slowly. Strip leaves from stalks when dry and store in sealed jars out of the light. Dried mint leaves will keep about a year.

Oregano

Oregano is a marjoram, and marjorams are members of the *Labiata* family, one of the largest of the herb groups. You will often find other types of oregano, with different Latin names, commonly called wild, or pot, marjoram. If you plant Greek oregano *(prismaticum)* you will have the variety most cooks and gardeners agree is true oregano.

This herb really needs no introduction if you grew up with Italian cooking or discovered a love of pizza that transcends your own ancestry.

Oregano can be used dried or fresh, from the garden or the windowsill, with tomatoes — especially tomato sauce with meat on spaghetti and with mushrooms. Meats that benefit from a sprinkling of oregano include sausage, lamb, pork and goose. You can also use it with eggs, especially in omelettes, and with vegetables like beans and cabbage. Oregano is a large part of the mixed spice called chili powder and it can be added to batters for fried foods or mixed with basil.

You can grow oregano from seed or from a transplant. It can be successful either way, and will keep growing or re-seed itself. You can propagate more by transplanting root sections from established plants or by transplanting cuttings. Oregano requires good, rich, deeply cultivated soil in a sunny spot. Regular watering is a must. Cutting oregano back before it flowers will make the plant bushy. Oregano dries well, so harvest often throughout the growing season.

Growing Oregano
- Seed or transplant nursery stock.
- Greek oregano is best choice.
- Needs good soil, sun, water.

Using Oregano
Dried or fresh in tomato and meat sauces, Italian, Spanish and Mexican cooking, fatty meats.

Take the stalks for drying when the flowers are blooming for maximum strength. Oregano is stronger dried than it is fresh — increase portions by one half if using fresh in a recipe that calls for dried oregano.

Except in milder climates, oregano is an annual, but mulching may help it get through your winter. If this technique is successful, cut back old growth in spring. It can be grown as a container plant, since it can stand the dry conditions in planters and indoor pots.

Three Ornamental Herbs: Nasturium, Marigold, Scented Geranium

Nasturtium, marigold and geranium are not often thought of as the names of herbs. But, using any of them can give your dishes, and your reputation as a gourmet chef, a real boost.

Nasturtium is a low growing or climbing plant that has bright flowers and round green leaves. But it becomes more than just a pretty flower when you use the leaves in salads and floating the flowers on consomme. You can pickle the flower buds in wine vinegar for use as a milder, less expensive, substitute for capers in Caesar salads, white sauces and fish recipes. Nasturtium flowers are also used in potpourri.

Marigold — the pot marigold variety is the best of the many — is a salad herb as well as an easy growing, colourful addition to your herb bed. Use the youngest leaves and petals for a spicy taste in salads and use the flower centre as a substitute for saffron in rice dishes. The colour is

Marigold

> **Using Flower Herbs**
> Flower blossoms, petals and seeds in food have been a gourmet
> secret for years, and their use is now exploding in popularity.

the same as saffron, the flavour is different. Saffron is a very expensive spice, marigold is not. Marigolds have an ancient reputation as a tea herb, but are not often used that way today. The colours of the petals make them ideal for potpourri.

Scented Geranium varieties will fill the herb bed with a heady array of fragrances and provide leaves to flavour jellies, puddings, stuffings and teas and to scent potpourri. Use them like any other herbal leaf — carefully at first. There is a wide range of scents: apple, rose, lime, peppermint, orange and lavender. Since geraniums are usually sold by their colours, you may have to look around for scented types.

These three flower herbs have a love of sun in common. Keep them out of the shade, especially in cooler zones. Scented geraniums are usually transplanted from nursery stock, and stem cuttings can be taken to expand the bed. Geraniums can be wintered over after blooming if they're pulled and kept cool and dry. Cut them back in the fall and repot them in the spring. Nasturiums and marigolds grow from seeds, planted after last frost, and need well drained sites. Pinch out the first bud or flower from marigolds to get a bunch of blooms. Use the youngest, most tender leaves from all these herbs.

Parsley

There are three types of parsley — French, or curly-leafed; Italian, a flat-leafed parsley; and Hamburg, a parsley grown for its white parsnip style root. Treat Hamburg like other root crops (carrots, beets, etc.) by giving it deeply worked, stone-free soil. Parsley is easy to grow in most places, but it really thrives in rich, well-fertilized, well-lighted soil. It can be started from seed inside your house eight weeks before last frost in spring and transplanted after the first frost. It can also be bought in flats, hardened off and set out after the last frost. Succession plantings of parsley will keep you well supplied through the summer. Northern zone gardeners don't usually have a problem with bolting (the herb going unexpectedly to seed), but cut off the central stem if you see a flower head developing. Harvest your parsley by taking the outside stalks. Parsley is a biennial plant but it is most often grown as an annual. Leaving it in the ground and letting it seed usually results in a crop the next year. Alternaitvely, it can be potted and brought inside, where it will continue to flourish if watered regularly and fertilized monthly.

Parsley

Use the fresh tops and stalks of your parsley plant when cooking. Parsley can be dried, but freezing is much better for preservation. The best option is to keep it growing indoors. Harvest Italian parsley leaves or stems and use them everywhere — green salads, cream cheese, fish soups, meat casseroles, fish and shellfish, poultry stuffings. You can also fry parsley or use it in biscuit mixes. Your choices are limited

---

Growing Parsley
- Seed and transplant or use bedding plants.
- Cut out flower heads.
- Many varieties available.

Using Parsley
Leaves, chopped fine or coarse, in practically all cooking. Use in *fines herbes, bouquet garni.*

only by your imagination or your recipe book — indeed one famous one says "There is practically no salad, meat or soup in which they (parsleys) cannot be used."

French cooking recipes that call for *bouquet garni* are really asking for two parts of parsley to one of bay (the leaf) and thyme. This mixture is usually stored in a cheesecloth bag tied with a string, which is removed before serving. When cooking with parsley, add it towards the end or the flavour is lost. Herb butters and *fines herbes* mixes call for parsley, chervil, chives, tarragon and sometimes basil, fennel, oregano or sage.

Rosemary

Legends tell us that rosemary is the herb of remembrance, love and fidelity, and that it only grows in the gardens of the righteous. This "old English" herb is actually Mediterranean in origin. It is grown more as a decorative plant, good for hedges and shrubbery, than than as a culinary herb.

Rosemary is a powerful herb — use it with caution and follow the recipe. You may find you need "1/4 leaf" or "1/8 teaspoon." Don't worry, these small amounts will add plenty of distinct flavour to your dishes.

Growing Rosemary
- Very slow from seed: use stock or cuttings.
- Needs full sun, light, well drained soil.
- Prune to control shape, growth.

Using Rosemary
Leaves, fresh or dried, in small quantities with meats, breads, dried in pot pourri and sachets.

Rosemary has a wide range of uses — try it in combination with sage and thyme on lamb roasts, crushed in bread and biscuit mixes, with chicken, potatoes, cauliflower and tomatoes and as a spice in fruit juices and marinades. Or throw it on the coals when barbecuing for a special flavour and aroma.

Rosemary also has many medicinal uses, and is often combined with lemon balm and lemon verbena in household remedies. It will also add a lemon or pine aroma to your garden.

Rosemary

Today, rosemary is most popular in potpourri mixes. The needle-like leaves are one of the basic herbs of the blend.

Rosemary is best grown from nursery stock or cuttings from established plants. It can be tip layered or rooted from a branch and then cut to transplant (see Growing Herbs chapter).

If your area's temperature drops below -20°C in the winter, rosemary can only be grown as an annual. There are many varieties and many flower colours. The smaller cultivars are suitable for container growing, so you can enjoy rosemary year round.

Sage

Sage is universally known from Thanksgiving turkey stuffing and western movies, so it's easy to miss other uses for this herb. Sage is good in poultry stuffing because it goes well with fatty foods, helping make them more digestable. The sage that the cowboys chase the little dogies through is actually another kind of herb, *Artemisia tridentata*, a wormwood. Culinary sage varieties include both broad- and narrow-leaved sages, purple sage, tri-colour leaved sage, low-growing sage and white-flowered sage.

Sage

This range gives you a great chance to use sages in your flower garden, because the blooms and aroma are so exciting. Growing sages is best done from transplants because sage seeds grow slowly. Some sages are more hardy than others — the same sage can be an annual or a perennial depending on where you live. Give the plant sandy soil that's more alkaline than acidic, make sure it has lots of nutrients and don't overwater.

Growing Sage
- Transplant into sandy soil.
- Avoid overwatering roots.
- Prune out old wood.

Using Sage
Mince leaves for stuffings or breads, use whole for meats. Can be used in potpourris.

Sage is more than a stuffing seasoning — experiment a bit and unleash it's other culinary qualities. Remember, sage is good with fatty foods, so why not try it with duck, chicken, rabbit, sausage, cheese and pork roasts. Lay fresh whole sage leaves over a roast, or stack lamb or pork chops in the refrigerator, with sage leaves between the meat, all day before grilling. Cook potatoes in hot oil in the bottom of a pan, with sage leaves and garlic cloves.

Sage leaves can be minced for use in stuffings and breads, but use them whole otherwise.

Sage can be dried or frozen, but it's best fresh.

Summer and Winter Savory

Summer savory is the best choice unless you garden in a coastal area. Winter savory is perennial near the seashore, and will provide leaves with a mild, peppery flavour through the cold winter months. Annual summer savory is more common inland. Its leaves can be dried or frozen, but fresh is best.

As sage is to poultry stuffing, savory is to beans, bean salads and lentil soup. Don't limit yourself with either savory — you'll find them useful with fish, roast pork, potatoes and tomatoes. Winter savory adds interest to economy dishes like stews, meatloaf and hamburger.

The two varieties are grown differently. Summer savory is direct seeded after the last frost of spring in rich, moist soil that gets full sun. Make sure you space it so you don't have

Growing Savory
- Summer: seed, moist, rich soil.
- Winter: transplant, sandy, drier soil.
- Both: Prune to control. Pinch flowers to continue leafing.

Using Savory
Summer: leaves with beans, potatoes and fish. Winter: leaves with stews, hamburger.

to thin it later in the growing season. Winter savory, which can also be treated as an annual, should be transplanted from nursery flats into sandy, less moist soil, also after the last frost, and after hardening off. Expect summer savory to grow to 45 cm (18 in.) and winter savory from 30-40 cm (12-16 in.). Winter savory is likely to be more bushy than the summer variety. Both can be used as border plants if pruned back — their aroma is pleasant. Container gardeners will find summer savory to be their best choice. Winter savory

Savory

will do best in a sheltered, but still sunny location, and heavy mulching may help it through the winter. Companion plant both types of savory with beans.

Cooking with savory is a subtle and complimentary art — it is often mixed with other herbs like basil, marjoram, oregano, sage and thyme. The leaves are used minced if fresh or thawed, crumbled if dried. Winter savory is generally stronger in flavour than summer savory, but both are delicate. When adding savory to fish, sauces and soups, wait until the later stages of cooking so the flavour doesn't disappear. You can season to taste this way. A savory herb butter can be used in cooking beans or be served with them, and savory is recommended with canned beans and green vegetables to take away the "canned" taste. When adding savory to dips and butters, let the mixture sit for several hours to let flavours blend before serving.

Tarragon

Tarragon is usually associated with French cooking. Its strong and distinct flavour is best known from tarragon wine vinegar, and it is the defining ingredient of bearnaise sauce. It can also be used on vegetables, tomatoes and chicken, seafood, soups and marinades.

You can grow French tarragon from nursery stock or from cuttings or root division. Cuttings are dipped in rooting solution, started in potting soil, and set out in spring. Root division should also be done in spring. Growing tarragon from seed isn't easy. Most tarragon seed sold in packets is Russian tarragon, which is considered an ornamental plant or a poor herbal substitute. Tarragon can thrive in poor, sandy soil, but will do better in rich soil. It does poorly in wet, poorly drained ground. It will grow to 60 cm (2 ft.) and maintenance pruning will provide cuttings for most kitchens. The plant should be renewed every three years. Tarragon is a perennial in warmer climates, but must be mulched in winter to survive severe temperatures. Tarragon can be grown indoors in light, sandy potting soil that isn't over-watered. A healthy tarragon plant has shiny, green leaves.

Tarragon can be used in potpourris, *fines herbes* mixes and butters. You can make tarragon wine vinegar by taking the leaves (always leave at least a third of the growth on the plant), washing and drying them well and adding them to a bottle of red, white or cider wine vinegar. Start taste testing after three days. You can use herbs preserved in the vinegar for cooking. Tarragon can also be used in herb salt.

Growing Tarragon
- From root division or cuttings.
- Needs dry but rich soil, good drainage.
- Mulch in winter.

Using Tarragon
Leaves whole or minced in French cooking, especially sauces, poultry, fish and shellfish. Used for tarragon wine vinegar.

Thyme

When you look for thyme, you'll discover many varieties. Stick to *Thymus vulgaris, citrodorus* or *herba-barona* for cooking. Creeping thymes are ground covers and border plants and aren't very useful in the kitchen. All thymes are annuals if not sold as hardy in your area.

Thyme

Give your thyme sun and a bit of space in good soil. Thyme can't stand competition for light and room, but it repays repays your kindness as one of the kitchens' most useful herbs.

Harvest cooking leaves when they're dry, and use them with meats, poultry, pasta and fish. Finely minced leaves can be sprinkled into stuffing, stew pots, or tea mixtures. Dried thyme can be stronger because its natural oils concentrate. Dried thyme is important in Manhattan clam chowders, and thyme, fresh or dried, is a good herb with any kind of fish.

Thyme is an easy first choice as a kitchen herb. *Thymus vulgaris* will grow through the winter as a house plant. In summer, it grows well in a rock garden setting. It's an easy care plant, grows from seed and is commonly available as a bedding plant. Pruning it encourages growth.

Growing Thyme
- Seed indoors, transplant, or use bedding plants.
- Usually low, bushy. Pruning helps shape, growth.
- Needs sun, space, good soil, little care.

Using Thyme
With meats, poultry, fish, stews, sauces. Good with other herbs, especially in teas.

Herbs in the Kitchen

Herbs are grown to be used. Although they're pleasant to have in the garden, we enjoy them most when we employ them in our meals.

One gourmet touch that starts in your herb garden is the use of herbs in making stock for either gravies or soups or as the basis for full-bodied stews and casseroles.

For good reason, many recipes call for a *bouquet garni* (see Glossary) — a tiny bag of herbs, usually containing parsley, bay leaf, thyme and another herb of your choice. The resulting liquid should be as free as possible of all extraneous materials. This is especially important in the making of clear soups.

It's embarrassing when one of your guests has to remove a piece of bay leaf from a dish. The same would be true for a thoroughly lifeless sprig of parsley or rosemary.

Many herbs, even in their fresh form, will virtually disintegrate during the boiling and lengthy simmering of a good stock and the vast majority will be caught in the sieve when the stock is strained.

Experienced cooks measure by instinct as much as cups, teaspoons and milligrams. Getting that experience, if you're new to the job, means taking it easy with herbs, spices — and all ingredients, for that matter — until you're sure. For starters, add very small amounts at a time until tasting and testing tells you the amount is right. It's always possible to add more, but it's very difficult to remove or hide an overdone flavouring. Remember that dried herbs, your own or commercially bottled, have a shelf life of no more than a year. After that, you need new ones.

Soup garnishes

A scattering of herbs on a bowl of soup can be both an eye-catching garnish and an aromatic highlight to the principal flavour.

Whenever possible, use fresh-picked herbs. Chopping or mincing herb leaves releases flavour best. To use the whole and still get the most benefit, crush the leaf between two spoons before dropping it into the soup. A spoonful can be floated in the middle of the soup bowl. Herbs can also be whipped into plain yogurt.

Vinegars

The best-known herb vinegar is without doubt tarragon vinegar, often known as tarragon wine vinegar. But basil, thyme, dill and nasturtiums also make good vinegars. The vinegar will pick up the colour of the herb as well as its flavour. Strong and mild herbs can be blended in vinegars.

To make herb vinegars, three or four well-leaved stems should be cut, washed and blotted dry to remove some moisture and concentrate the flavour. These are simply placed in a bottle of white wine vinegar. Be sure to follow these rules:

- don't use a metal cap on the bottle
- make sure the vinegar covers all the herbs
- shake the mixture daily for the first week
- then shake once a week until vinegar is to taste
- keep the mixture in a warm, sunny place

Taste test regularly and remove the herbs— you can use them in recipes— when the taste is right. It may take weeks for the herb's flavour to completely penetrate the vinegar.

Medieval Cooks

Oils

Production of herb oils closely mirrors that of herb vinegars. Each herb should be fresh cut before being immersed in a high-quality salad or olive oil.

Strong herbs like sweet marjoram, peppermint and garlic can be used for herb oils. Keep the finished oil in dark coloured bottles. Herb oils should not be used for general cooking. They are best used in oil and vinegar salad dressings and in certain spiced bread and bun recipes.

Butters

You probably already know about garlic butter — but why not try your own herb butters with tarragon or chives?

Start with butter at room temperature, so it's slightly soft. Add fresh herb leaves, chopped fine, and stir. Some things to remember — a tablespoon of fresh herb will flavour 250 ml (1/4 lb.) of butter, margarine can be used, and unsalted butter will take the herb flavour better than salted. That's all the recipe you need. Herbs that taste great in butters include parsley, chives, basil, tarragon, rosemary and lemon thyme. Herb butters should be kept chilled and can be used on anything you'd use regular butter on or in.

Herb salts can also be used to flavour sour cream for home-made chip and vegetable dips, honey for teas, or salts. To make your own herb salts, use non-iodized or sea salt and fresh, minced leaves. The mixture should be one-to-one and blending is the quickest way to do the mixing. Dry the mixture on a cookie sheet in a 90°C/200°F oven, bottle tightly and keep in a dark, cool, dry place.

Sauces

Italians love pesto and use it in many ways. A home-maker will frequently make a fairly large quantity and store it in jars, sealed with the finest olive oil, or freeze it.

If you do not have a pestle and mortar, the paste-making stage can be achieved in a food processor or blender.

First, puree about 1/2 teaspoonful of salt with two peeled cloves of garlic and 25 g (1 oz.) of pine nuts.

Now add 25 g (1 oz.) of freshly grated real parmesan cheese (if available, otherwise use processed) and 50 g (2 oz.) of freshly picked basil leaves and blend these briefly. Begin to add, drop by drop, a good olive oil. The mixture will soon take on the texture of mayonnaise.

Pesto was designed with pasta in mind. It also makes a memorable change as a topping for baked potatoes. People who get hooked on this sauce can find an incredible number of reasons to use it.

French remoulade sauce is used on cold beef cuts, cooked fish and egg dishes. Use it on root vegetables or cold chicken for a different reaction to a standard dish.

Combine 300 mL (1/2 pt.) of mayonnaise and 15 mL (1 tbsp.) each of finely chopped tarragon, chervil or chives, parsley, gherkins, and Dijon (or Hot or French) mustard, with 10 mL (1 tsp.) of chopped capers and two canned anchovies, chopped and mashed.

Dill sauce can be made quickly and does not need to mature for any length of time.

In a clean jar put 30 mL (2 tbsp.) of olive oil, 60 mL (4 tbsp.) of reconstituted lemon juice and 30-45 mL (2-3 Tbsp) of fresh and finely chopped dill. Add a half teaspoonful of salt and fresh ground black pepper to taste. Shake the contents well and chill if desired.

Bay leaves can be used in sauces.

Dill sauce is excellent with fresh-sliced English cucumbers. It should be drizzled over a decorative arrangement of cucumber slices and allowed to chill before serving.

Teas

Tea from herb leaves is a traditional drink and has a place in history, in medicine and in the home. Mints, lemon herbs and German chamomile are the most popular tea herbs. Borage, dill seeds, fennel leaves, lovage, marigold, marjoram, rosemary, sage and thyme will also make tasty teas that will be different and refreshing. All herb teas are made in exactly the same way as tea from a bag. Use small quantities of fresh leaves, one or two to a cup to start (only two teaspoons of dried, powdered herb), and boiling water. Herb teas should steep about three minutes before you start sipping. Herb teas are usually sweetened to taste — try using honey.

Herb teas are often made from blends. Some herbs, usually mints and the lemon herbs, are mixed with commercial teas to make unique-tasting drinks.

Saffron for tea.

Parsley Wine

This is an old-country recipe about which there is one peculiarity — it used to be made in considerable quantities by people who were proud abstainers yet had this benign idea that wine made of parsley could not possibly be intoxicating.

In fact, parsley wine that has been made with care and patience can be a drink of amazing potency.

Place 1/2 kg (about 1 lb.) of parsley tops (remove as much stem as possible) in a large bowl and pour 4.5 L (1 gal.) of boiling water over them. Cover the bowl with cheesecloth and allow the mixture to steep for a full 24 hours.

Take 2 large oranges and 2 large lemons and remove their rind. Remove as much pith as possible.

Strain the parsley juice into a fresh bowl and add to it the citrus rinds, cut generously into slivers and add 25 g (1 oz.) of cubed peeled ginger stem. Bring the contents to a boil and add 1.8 kg (4 lb.) of sugar. Allow to simmer for 5 minutes. Meanwhile, in the original bowl, squeeze the juice from the oranges and lemons. Now pour the simmered liquid over the citrus juices and allow to cool.

Before the liquid cools, float a slice of toast, spread with 420 g (14 oz.) of fresh yeast (or one package of activated yeast), on the surface of the mixture.

Cover this pan with cheesecloth and allow fermentation to do its work. This will take four to seven days.

At the end of this time, having strained the liquid through a sieve lined with cheesecloth or muslin, bottle the wine. Use tops that will allow gases from any remaining fermentation to escape.

Finally, when there is no evidence (bubbles) of any further fermentation, cork the bottles and store them, preferably on a rack, in a cool dark place.

Three months is a reasonable time for aging. The longer the wine is left, the more character it will assume.

Potpourri

Potpourri (pronounced po-poo-REE) is a popular combination of rose petals and herb leaves, other flower petals and preservatives. It recalls the days when herbs were important for their strong and clean scents. Today, they're a pleasant accent, not a necessary mask.

If you want to make potpourris, begin with planting planning — while a few herbs of each variety might supply a kitchen, potpourris use large quantities of dried flowers, and you'll need a bigger herb garden. Similarly, choose fragrant varieties of roses, rose geraniums and carnations. Blossoms for potpourris should be collected just as they open and should be dried slowly and thoroughly. Most recipes will call for quarts of rose petals and pints or cups of herb leaves and flowers.

Every potpourri needs a fixative and an aromatic oil. These are best bought from craft stores, although the Florentine iris or orris root can be grown in the milder zones. The root is dug, scrubbed and dried, then ground and powdered. Other fixatives are tonka bean oil, gum benzoin or citrus fruit peels.

A simple potpourri is a bowl of dried lavender flowers. More elaborate pot pourris use a wide variety of fragrant flower and herb blossoms, fixatives and oils.

Here is a simple rose and herb potpourri that most gardens can grow (all quantities are of dried flowers):

1 L (1 qt.) of rose petals
1 L (1 qt.) of lavender flowers
500 mL (1 pt.) of rose geranium flowers.
Optionally: 500 mL (1 pt.) rosemary leaves, chamomile
*   flowers, marigolds, or lilac.*
45 mL (3 tbsp.) ground orris root fixative
30 mL (2 tbsp.) each of cinnamon, allspice and cloves.
15 g (1/2 oz.) essential oil of your choice: rose, orange,
*   sandalwood are common.*

Mix the dried flowers and other ingredients together with your hands and then cover and store unopened for a month in a cool, dry place. Use glass or ceramic containers for potpourri in your house, and make sure that you don't use metal utensils at all in preparing your mixtures.

Potpourri mixtures, if ground to a coarse powder, can be sewn into sachets, which are handy in clothes hampers, closets, drawers and as gifts. Use a dash of brandy to revive a faded potpourri aroma, or mix in newer dried flowers, using the old mix as bulk.

Many craft shops offer potpourri mixes to which you can add your own garden herb flowers.

Growing Herbs

Herbs are relatively easy to grow. Most kinds prefer lots of sun. Many originally developed on sandy, dry soils in hot sunny climates, but overall they thrive in a soil rich in nutrients that is neither too alkaline nor too acidic. The alkalinity or acidity is measured on a pH scale of 14, on which 7.0 is neutral. Most gardeners will have a soil that is about right, providing it has had compost or dried manures dug into it. The vast majority of herbs and most garden crops do best in 5.5 to 7.5 pH soil. Good herb soil should be sufficiently brittle to maintain a reasonable degree of air entrapment — so that oxygen is available in the soil for the micro-organisms that nourish plant growth.

If in doubt about your soil's pH, you can buy soil testing equipment at a good garden centre or horticultural store, or contact your state or provincial agriculture department for details on soil testing. Cultivation of the garden and constant attention to returning organic matter through addition of compost and manures will improve every type of soil. Crop rotation, even of your herbs, and succession planting, with fertilizing during growth, will repay your efforts with far better yields, healthier plants and a longer growing season.

What herbs require

Most herbs require sandy soil for best growing results. Soil is considered sandy if it is made up of 50 per cent or more sand (defined as particles from 1/250 in. to 1/12 in.) mixed with clay (particles smaller than 1/50,000 in.) and silt (particles between clay and 1/500 in.). Sandy does not mean beach-like — soil must always be a combination of growing

matter. If your soil contains more than 50 per cent clay and silt, it is a clay soil, and should be amended (see Glossary) with garden sand for herb growing. Container gardening will allow you to custom blend your soil for specific herbs, if your regular soil is a problem. To get a rough idea of your gardens' soil composition, separate 250-500 ml (1/2 to 1 cup) of your soil, just like you'd separate fat from meat juices for a gravy. Mix the soil with 750-1,500 mL of water and let it settle overnight in a clear drinking glass or jar. Looking across the contours in your cup, you will see the largest sand at the bottom and the finest clays at the top. You can estimate the proportions easily. "Ideal" garden soil is a 40 per cent sand, 40 per cent silt, 20 per cent clay mix, but herbs can use a more sandy mix. Remember, herbs will not necessarily take kindly to neglect. They need adequate watering and an occasional top-dressing of an all-purpose fertilizer to thrive.

Drainage is important for healthy herbs — few survive in wet or soggy soil. Overwatering can be a source of the problem, but more often, soil composition is to blame.

Fertilizers

A well-balanced soil is rich in a variety of nutrients. Fertilizers simply supplement what nature provides in the soil, or replenishes the supply when we demand too much in terms of growth or take too many crops.

Fertilizers can be divided into two groups — organic and inorganic. Organic fertilizers are obviously of organic origin — blood, hoof, horn and bone meals, fish meals and sewage sludge or slurry or many other sources. Their virtue is that they are slow acting, and add humus to the soil as decomposition takes place. Inorganic fertilizers are mainly produced from mineral sources. It makes no difference to the plant how the elements are produced.

Fertilizers are labelled according to their content of varying amounts of three elements essential to growth — Nitrogen (N), Phosphorus (P), and Potash (K). They may contain additional trace amounts of minerals like boron or magnesium, which are also important.

Nitrogen is necessary to maintain a healthy supply of plant proteins responsible for a vigorous production of stems and leaves. Phosphorus develops the root system's ability to absorb the nutrients in the soil. Phosphorus is also vital to both the maturing and fruiting or flowering of plants. Potash (or potassium) is a chemical imperative if a plant is to resist disease and to keep its root system lively.

A good garden centre will give you reliable recommendations. For herbs, look for "slow release" fertilizers with low potencies. These allow you to feed plants without "burning" roots or overstimulating growth, and they let the plant draw the fertilizer it needs during the season. "Balanced" fertilizers will be the safest blends for the new gardener to use — a 6-6-6 labelling or similar is ideal. Mid- and late-season fertilizing should usually be lower in nitrogen, or higher in potassium and potash. Nitrogen is used for growth and is ususally unneccessary during this period.

Natural fertilizers like composted steer or mushroom manures also have a lot of usable organic material that makes them doubly useful.

What to grow and how to harvest

What to grow is a question of chef's choice — it's your kitchen, it's your garden. Herb standards, such as parsley, sage, thyme and chives, should be a component of any herb garden. Many of your other choices will be easy, depending on your diet, favourite foods or ethnic background. The 26

herbs in this book are all generally popular and useful, and are recommended for gardeners and cooks everywhere.

One thing a cook will quickly discover when he or she plucks a few leaves or a sprig from a fresh plant is that the smell or aroma is more noticeable, and gives more zest to a dish than the dried herbs used in so many kitchens.

Unfortunately, many 'perennial' herbs will not over-winter in northern climates. You might be successful with a few of the woody perennials if you cover them with a thick layer of straw or compost before the ground freezes. Don't expect them to survive prolonged periods of severe cold. You will also see some references to herbs as "perennials grown as annuals." These *may* be hardy depending on where you live, but local conditions will determine that.

Some of the herbs described in this book will continue to grow if brought inside for the winter, though generally with varying results. Indoor herbs need lots of light and may require some cutting back to reduce their nutritional needs. Many tender perennials can best be grown year round by keeping them in larger-sized clay pots, burying them in the garden in summer, and cleaning off the pots and bringing them indoors for fall and winter. Herbs grown this way will

While innumerable medicinal benefits are attributed to herbs, infusions and teas should only be made according to time-tested recipes. Vast amounts of myth and folklore surround herbs, and many magical healing qualities are described but never proven.

Any self-medication may simply prolong a condition and worsen the problem before professional attention is sought. Never try to make a herbal tea replace a prescription medicine.

require extra watering and fertilizing attention.

Rosemary is a good example. If the temperature drops below freezing in the winter, rosemary should be grown in a pot and brought indoors until spring. It needs light and humidity. In spring, it can be set outside again. Since rosemary is a slow-growing herb with a bushy form, it must be regarded as an annual if it cannot be protected.

Some common herbs, like bay, are simply not hardy in Canada and northern United States. Bay can be an expensive, difficult herb to grow, but if given a large pot, with a superior soil mix and a reliable overhead light source, it may supply you with ample amounts of it's inimitable leaves for stocks, soups and stews. For the frost-free part of the year, a bay will develop new growth if replanted in the garden.

Harvesting and Storing

What do you do with plants that are abundantly productive during the summer months, but tend to die in the fall? Herbs can be harvested at any time during their growth season, as long as you don't completely strip the plant. As a rule, always leave at least a third of the growth when you harvest.

The most obvious form of harvesting is fresh-for-the-pot. A rule of thumb — you should add twice the quantity of fresh herbs to a recipe that has assumed you will be using dried herbs. If in doubt about the amount needed, use the recipe and adjust to taste. Individual cooks and gardeners sometimes disagree with each other whether fresh herbs are stronger than dried herbs. It becomes a matter of taste and personal preference. Herbs get their flavours from their oils — the stronger the herb flavour (rosemary, tarragon, sage, oregano) the less the cook needs to adjust between dried and fresh.

Annual herbs should be harvested at their peak, definitely before the first frost in the fall. The simplest way to preserve them is to cut their stems and hang them in a dry place with good air circulation. Fine-leaved herbs such as sage, thyme and rosemary should be enclosed in a muslin bag, cheesecloth or even the perforated plastic bags used by some supermarket bakeries for oven-fresh breads. You can also dry herbs by leaving them on a newspaper or on a large pizza pan in a warm oven overnight. Take the oven to 350°F/175°C, turn it off and set in the herbs. You can also use a microwave oven for quick drying. Lay tarragon, basil, marjoram, savory, sage, thyme or mint leaves between cloth or paper towel, and try a low setting for two to four minutes or 30 seconds on high. A few tries will give you the best settings for your oven. Stems of herbs can be dried the same way and then ground up with a blender for a coarse powder that can be used in a *bouquet garni* bag. Very thick herbs should be air dried before microwave drying.

Air drying is the ages-old way to preserve herbs. In this method, herbs are harvested, stems and all, and bunched. Most herbs are strongest flavoured just before flowering and this is the ideal time to harvest them. Whether you'll be using leaves or flowers, take the whole stalk, clipping the herb off at ground level. This is best done in the morning, after the dew is gone but before the sun has become strong. The herb oils will be strongest then — after the sun hits, they start to evaporate.

Herbs should be air-dried upside down, hanging in bunches in an airy, dry and warm spot. This may not be easy to arrange. Attics, if available, are good choices, but they are sometimes too warm — over 90°F/32°C is not recommended. Basements can be too cool and occasionally damp.

Herbs need space to dry. A clothes dryer rack, an arrangement of hangers in a closet or a shed or garage may be

Gardening and Making Chaplets

workable choices. Cover the floor to catch leaves and seeds. Drying seed herbs like dill and fennel inside paper bags helps catch the seeds but slows drying. Do not use plastic bags for this procedure.

Your herbs are dry when they crumble easily. Strip the leaves off stalks and store. Glass or plastic jars, plastic bags or containers, or preserving jars are best for storage. Whatever is used should be airtight and stored away from sunlight. Any sign of mold on dried herbs indicates they were still damp when stored. Re-dry them, or try again with new herbs. If space or time is a problem, microwave drying is an option.

The latest development in preserving herbs is flash freezing, which extracts moisture very quickly at extremely low temperatures. Refrigerator freezer compartments act relatively slowly and in the process create comparatively large ice crystals which break down the cellular structure of the herb. Frozen herbs should be used immediately — chopped or cooked while frozen. Preserving systems that seal food in plastic with heat, or that draw out air from the package, will preserve herbs and their flavours more efficiently. Store frozen herbs in small quantities to minimize waste.

Let's get gardening

Getting the raw materials for a herb garden is easy — start from seed or buy a well-developed seedling or young plant from a reputable garden centre or a favourite farmer's market stall. But you must still choose between indoor and outdoor growing, and decide which plants will be best in which spot.

Starting from seed is simple — follow the instructions printed on the packet and provide a growing environment that fits the plant's needs. Since many herb seeds are extremely fine, mixing them with an equal amount of sand may make distribution, or drilling, more even. Most packets contain far more seeds than you need, but seeds can keep for several years in a sealed jar in a refrigerator.

Seeding can be done in three ways: directly into the soil

where the plant is to grow, from flats or trays for later transplant, or from peat pots or pellets for later transplant. The latter method works best for plants with sensitive root systems, like fennel, and allows you to transplant the entire pot without disturbing the delicate taproots. Transplants should be performed after the last frost of the winter. The indoor seeding dates for transplanted or potted herbs should be well ahead of your last frost date, and seedlings should be hardened off before being set out.

Many herbs, like scented geraniums and rosemary,

are slow or unlikely to grow from seed and are best grown from bedding plants or cuttings. Established young plants give the northern-climate gardener a great start on the outdoor growing season. A garden centre can give new gardeners a good start and a suggest a suitable variety of herbs for the local climate — if an herb is not sold as a bedding plant in your climate zone, it may not be hardy. Beware of "leggy" herbs — tall, thin plants, that have had too little light. They will rarely become compact, healthy plants.

More and more herbs are started in bio-degradable peat moss packs, which make transplanting simple. Don't try to remove plants from peat or pellet packs— too much root damage is done. Pressed paper or fibre packs look very similar — know what you are buying. Similarly, ask if the plants must be hardened off (see Glossary) before planting. If they are just out of a greenhouse, this will be vital. Be sure the ground into which you transplant your herbs is prepared — well forked and well manured so that the root system can begin immediate development. Water in well and protect from frost for the first weeks.

Plastic starter pots are vulnerable to drying out at this critical beginning-growth stage and herbs bought in such pots should be given a precautionary soaking before being transplanted. If you're new to gardening or in a new garden, "transplanting solutions" or "seed starters" sold in garden centres are good insurance.

Growing herbs indoors

Since we like to eat all year, and spring and summer can be the shortest seasons, indoor herb gardening can carry us over the months when our regular garden is under the snow.

It is also the obvious way for apartment and condo gardeners to raise their own herbs. Most herbs will do well in indoor settings if enough of their needs can be met. The exceptions might be larger herbs like mint, lovage and fennel, but even these can be grown in large pots indoors if enough space and light can be provided. Some herbs, like bay, are indoor plants only for northern gardeners.

Many herbs — like chives and parsley — can thrive indoors and out. Since they, like many other herbs, don't dry well, they are good herbs to grow fresh all year round. These two are easy to "pot up" at the end of a season and bring indoors, where they will carry on growing if given a window-sill or other well-lighted southern exposure.

Some herbs should be potted all year round because they are tender and won't survive a frost. Keeping them in pots allows you to remove them from your garden without root shock, but lets them maintain good growth in the summer months. When bringing any outdoor growing plant indoors for winter, remember to spray it for disease and pests at least a week ahead of moving time. Pot it outside and leave it there for a while to adapt to the pot. If some root is lost, cut back the above ground parts by an equal amount. If you're using old clay pots, sterilize them before potting in a new plant. Soak the pot in a mix of one part household bleach to 10 parts water for half an hour, and rinse well.

Keep outdoor/indoor plants away from indoor or house-plants to avoid the spread of disease and pests. Most herbs will continue to produce useful leaves throughout the winter if treated like a houseplant and fertilized regularly. Indoor herbs won't be as prolific as outdoor herbs, and regular cutting back will be necessary to encourage new leaf growth and maintain shape.

Watering requires care — many herbs can't tolerate overwatering or constantly wet soil. Make sure the top inch of potting soil is dry before the next watering so the roots won't get soggy and the drown the plant. Good drainage out of the bottom of any pot is vital.

Repotting may be necessary for some herbs if they become rootbound. A rootbound plant has a thick outside wrap of small roots when the plant is turned out of the pot. Separate those roots so they are loose from the soil, give the plant a pot one size larger and add new planting mix and fertilizer. Remember to water the plant after repotting.

Some herbs, like dill and fennel, are fast, efficient growers anywhere, while others, like parsley, grow best when directly seeded where they will grow. Most herbs can be started indoors and transplanted after the danger of frost is past. That last frost date is variable everywhere. If you don't know it, a neighbour with a garden, the local agriculture extension or county agent, a university or college agriculture information department or a seed catalog may provide the date. It's

essential, because your success will depend on starting the seeds early enough so that they are ready to transplant soon after the last frost, and late enough so that they don't outgrow your seed flats while there's still snow on the ground.

If you're growing herbs year round indoors, start them in pots large enough to keep them in when full grown. Use sterilized potting soil, and maintain them in a place where they can be warm and get at least 6 hours of light every day. Indoor herbs need good quality soil and lots of fertilizer to continue to produce useful leaves. If light is a problem, they need a grow light, a mix of cool and warm fluorescent lamps or of cool fluorescent and incandescent (bulb) lamps. However, they can't thrive if the lights are on 24 hours a day — they also need a resting period. Indoor herbs should grow healthy, aromatic leaves, be a good colour, and have firm, sturdy stalks. If they look sickly, suspect overwatering, lack of fertilizing, lack of light, or being rootbound as problems first and correct the condition.

An empty closet or storeroom makes an excellent indoor herb garden. A timer on the lighting system, a large, deep planter box, sturdy bench or sawhorses for support, some fertilizer and a watering can are all you need for a convenient indoor herb garden that won't clutter up your living space.

Indoor starting for herbs is economical and efficient in colder zones, where commercial bedding plants may be limited in selection or just not affordable. Buying seed packets by mail provides the greatest number and selection of plants at the least expense. Seeds can be stored up to a year if kept dry.

You can test the germination capacity of your stored seeds by laying a sample ten seeds on a damp paper towel, kept between two saucers (the top one overturned) in a warm dry spot. If fewer than three seeds sprout or show signs of life within two weeks, plant extras, or buy new seeds. Start most indoor herbs under lights as you would houseplants, but keep the lights close — no more than 30 cm (12 in.) away from the soil surface — until seeds have sprouted. Remember, that some herbs, like parsley, must be kept in darkness until they sprout.

Indoor planting follows the same rules as outdoor planting — cover the seeds only with the depth of soil suggested and mist the water on. Having a greenhouse top (or plastic cover) for the seed flats will retain soil moisture in parts of the continent with low humidity.

Because most cooks don't need a lot of herb plants, even a small indoor herb garden will grow enough for a kitchen. Balcony boxes should be cultivated like potted plants — remember to keep a close watch on soil quality, fertilization, watering and diseases. In winter, bring your herbs inside or keep them close to the walls and insulate the sides of your balcony boxes. Add light if needed, and trim overgrown plants. Some shrubby herbs will need to be cut back, sometimes to just above ground level, because their woody stems stop producing leaves. Rosemary and tarragon, lavender and thyme are prone to this. Many indoor and balcony plants grow out toward the light, especially on northern windows. Rotate the pots to keep growth even and upright. Too little light will result in tall, floppy plants with widely spaced leaves on their stalks.

Herbs
Through the Ages

Whether it's the middle of winter or summer, gardeners are always thinking of ways to expand their plots. One of the easiest, most enjoyable and most varied ways to do this is to introduce herbs to the tomato, bean and pea staples. Herbs are a natural choice for both the beginner and the pro.

The Bible is richly sown with the names of herbs. Even before the writing of the Old Testament, Chinese scholars documented, for medicinal purposes, a herb for whatever ails you through every day of the year. Traces of herbs have been found in the earliest human settlements.

The Romans took their herbs on their conquests, for medical purposes and for flavouring foods. In this way, herbs that first grew around the Mediterranean eventually came to North America from Britain, France and Spain. All are former Roman colonies.

In the Middle Ages, herbs were used in prodigious quantities to mask the taste of game or fish gone bad. Herbs covered the odours of communities where sewage systems were non-existent, and were used in potions to relieve aches and pains, to correct blood disorders, and to try to cure what we now recognize as serious clinical ailments. Monastery gardens preserved the herbs and the monks and nuns of the

A Sick Man in Bed

church tended their plots with extraordinary care. As well, the teachings developed at these monasteries about herbs and their medical properties were spread far and wide.

Herbs remained important through the upheavals of history. With the invention of printing came books called herbals — collections of real and mythical knowledge about herbs that were as important as Bibles to the people of that era. The Renaissance, civil wars and the Industrial Revolution came and went, but herbs remained an important part of people's livese. With the creation of great estates, a breed of master gardeners began to develop formal gardens, which would invariably include a herb garden, geometrically laid out and bordered with clipped hedges. Elegance and utility were combined in the cultivation of herbs because they were essential to life. While kitchens made continuous demands on herb production, the upper classes were aware that to smell sweet was attractive. Sachets of herbal leaves and seeds were placed between bed linen and worn in little purses. Herbs and spices served a vital role in disguising the smell of unwashed humanity and open sewers.

Medicinal history

Medicine began with botany, which is the study of plants. The sources of most early medicines were herbs. A garden was an important part of every home, great or humble, simply because the herbs provided the flavouring, the pre-servatives, and often much of the food, especially in the spring when they were mixed with the salad greens.

Herbal medicine remained important through the Second World War and herbs today are still a major source of pharmaceutical ingredients. Herbs as a food source lacked the glamour of modern packaging, and faded from everyday knowledge. However, good sense and good cooking have brought them back again. Herbs will always be a useful, pleasant, exciting, natural and renewable way to improve the taste and value of our food and the pleasure of our meals.

Glossary

Amending soil

Changing the composition of a soil by adding sand, manure, compost, peat or similar organic matter to improve its texture. It also refers to changing a soil's pH level by adding lime or bone meal.

Bouquet garni

A term that originated in French recipes and applies to the making clear soups and stocks. The bouquet of flavours, usually comprising a bay leaf, a sprig of parsley, a little sage and maybe some thyme or rosemary is parcelled in a bag of muslin and the string left trailing outside the pot so that it can be easily removed.

Compost

Natural fertilizer and soil conditioner made from organic materials such as leaves, weeds, lawn cuttings and dead plants. Household scraps such as vegetable trimmings and even egg shells can be added to compost, but not meats, bones or fats. Nature will break yopur compost down into an almost odourless, friable material, if it is piled compactly, turned regularly and kept moist. Compost should be dug into borders prior to seeding or planting. Rye broadcast in the fall as a cover crop and similarly forked into the soil, also enriches the soil.

Companion Planting

This is the practise of planting different species together to protect one or both from disease or to encourage growth. This method of planting is widely practised, but its benefits are still 'not proven' in plant science circles. Many plants should not be close together and these cases are well documented. See the text for each herb for more information on planting conflicts.

Condiment

Literally a seasoning — a fine powder or grain such as salt, pepper and mustard.

Cuttings

Sections of a woody herb best taken in mid-summer from half-ripened wood — a side shoot from the main stem without much bark. A cutting should be at least 7.5 cm (3 in) long. Cuttings should have some leaves but no flowers or buds. After dipping in a root hormone powder, place well-spaced cuttings in sterilized potting soil, or perlite. It must be kept moist. To retain a humid environment for your tray or pot, enclose it in a plastic bag. Rooting time varies but is indicated by new growth in the cutting.

Fines herbes

Mixture of chervil, chives, tarragon and occasionally other herbs with parsley as a constant. These herbs are finely chopped or minced, mixed together and used in a variety of recipes, especially in egg dishes and sauces. Fresh herbs are usually used if a recipe calls for *fines herbes*.

Growing from seed

Prepare your seed bed with lots of forking and raking to ensure a soil that's well aerated and free of lumps. Create a trench in this surface for the exact depth your seeds require. This is usually specified on the seed packet. A general rule of thumb is to plant no deeper than four times the seeds' width. Cover the seeds with fine soil and water with a mist spray. Many herb seeds are so minute you might get better distribution by pre-mixing them with fine sand. When the first leaves seem well established, the rows should be thinned to about 15 cm (6 in) between each seedling. Seeds grown in pots indoors should be in a sterilized potting mixture.

Hardening off

Bedding plants should be allowed to adjust to the garden climate from the greenhouse or indoor location in which they are raised. They should be set out, in shade, for several hours each day. Increase the time outside by an hour a day, but do not set out if there is any danger of frost. A week is usually adequate hardening off time before planting.

Hardiness

This is a rating of a plant's ability to stand winter cold. Both Agriculture Canada and the United States Department of Agriculture publish maps of hardiness zones. Information is available from District Agriculturalists (Canada) or County Extension offices (U.S.). Generally, hardiness determines whether a plant will be an annual or perennial in your zone. Most herbs are not perennial below zone 4 in Canada and zone 3 in the US. Local conditions vary greatly and cultivation practises like mulching also affect plant survival.

Infusion

Essentially the same process as described in the making of herb tea. The usual prescription was one wine-glass — you can safely convert to half a tea-cup. If it's a good night's sleep you're after, you should 'drink before retiring.'

Herb oil

Certain beauty preparations and astringents call for rose water and other distillates. Making them may to be too challenging for the average home-owner but the way to do it is as follows: Pick a fair amount of flower petals or herb leaves and soak ion proof spirit for up to two weeks. Then, using a kettle that is dispensable, attach a rubber hose to its spout and keep the liquid boiling vigorously. At some point part of the tubing should be immersed in ice-cold water. At the end of the tubing a jar will collect your herb oil drop by drop.

Mulch

A covering over the soil surrounding herbs and vegetables to inhibit weed growth and retain soil moisture. Grass cuttings will do the trick, although they tend to decompose into a mat which eventually has to be teased and distributed with a fork. Most perennials should be mulched for winter. More and more gardeners use black garbage bags, spread open with appropriate slits for the young plants. Black, of course, absorbs the heat from the sun, and keeps the soil moist and warm.

Oils

These are the essential ingredients that carry the characteristics of a particular herb. Even though they can be synthetically reproduced, natural herb oils are still very valuable to the soap and perfume industry.

Potpourri

A mixture of crushed herb leaves and flower petals (e.g. rose and, because they retain their colour, Geraniums) that will gently perfume a room for months. To retain their potency the ingredients of your potpourri should be 'fixed' in either sea salt or the dried and powdered peel of any citrus fruit. Then, in order to allow the fragrances to marry and mature, keep them in a sealed bottle for a few weeks before scattering into a pretty dish or sewing into a nicely embroidered sachet.

Scented waters

These are easily produced. As with tea, leaves are dropped into boiling water. But for scented waters, the leaves should be simmered for about 10 minutes. To increase the potency, add a shot of brandy or whisky. Have fun experimenting with combinations. Scented waters are excellent for making a bath a truly refreshing and unique occasion.

Spices

While in general herbs are valued for their leaves, spices are seeds, used whole (as in peppercorns, Caraway, Poppy and Cloves) or finely ground. But they can also be derived from a plant's ground root, from tree bark (Cinnamon) and from the outer casing of Nutmeg from which you get Mace. Other examples include Capers, Cloves, Cardomon, Tumeric and Saffron.

Tisane

A French word often used for a herbal tea made from fresh herb parts.

Other Reading

The Food Lovers Garden. Angelo M. Pellegrini. Lyons & Burford, New York, 1970.

Macmillan Book of Natural Herb Gardening. Kreuter (trans:Ray) Collier Macmillan, New York, 1985.

UBC Guide to Gardening in British Columbia. Maureen Garland, ed., UBC Botanical Garden, 1990.

Wild Teas, Coffees and Cordials. Hilary Stewart, Douglas and McIntyre, 1981.

Herbs. How To Select, Grow and Enjoy. Lathrop, Norma Jean, HP Books, Los Angeles, 1981 7th ed.

Foolproof Planting. Halpin,Anne Moyer, Rodale Press, Emmaus,PA. 1990.

Herbs. How to grow them and how to use them. Webster, Helen Noyes, Branford, Newton, MASS., 1959.

Sunset Western Garden Book. Clark, ed. Sunset Books, 1974.

Complete Book of Herbs and Spices. Lowenfield, Claire and Back, Phillipa, G.P.Putnams, New York, 1974.

Herb Garden, The. Sarah Garland, Penguin Books, 1984.

Taylor's Encyclopedia of Gardening. (fourth Ed) Norman Taylor, ed. Houghton Mifflin, 1976.

Herbs and the Fragrant Garden. Margaret Brownlow, Darton, Longman and Todd,London, rev. ed. 1978.

Gardening in Toronto. Pat Tucker, Lone Pine, Edmonton, 1991.

Harrowsmith Northern Gardener, The. Jennifer Bennet, Camden House, Toronto, 1982.

Carrots Love Tomatoes. Louise Riotte, McKenzie edition, Garden Way Books. 1987.

Jean Anderson Cooks. Jean Anderson, Morrow, New York, 1982.

Joy of Cooking. Rombauer Becker, Thomas Allen, Toronto, 1967.

Illustrated Herbal, The. Wilfrid Blunt and Sandra Raphael, Thames and Hudson (US ed) New York, 1979.

Rodale Herb Book, The. William Hylton, Ed., Rodale Press,1974.

Gardeners Hint Book, The. Charles L. Wilson, Johnathan David Publishers, Middle Village, N.Y. 1978.

Proven Tips for Lazy Gardeners. Linda Tilgner, Storey Communications, Mackenzie Edition. 1978.

Square Foot Gardening. Mel Bartholomew. Rodale Press, 1981.

Herbs for the Mediaeval Household. Margaret B. Freeman. The Metropolitan Museum of Art, 1943.

Other Homeworld Titles

Attracting Birds

ISBN 0-919433-87-1   64 pp.   5 1/2 x 8 1/2 $6.95

Balcony Gardening

ISBN 0-919433-98-7   64 pp.   5 1/2 x 8 1/2 $6.95

Jams and Jellies

ISBN 0-919433-90-1   48 pp.   5 1/2 x 8 1/2 $4.95

Pickles and Preserves

ISBN 0-919433-88-X   48 pp.   5 1/2 x 8 1/2 $4.95

Available in October, 1992

Breadmaking

ISBN 1-551050016-1   64 pp.   5 1/2 x 8 1/2 $6.95

Christmas Survival Guide

ISBN 1-55105-019-6   64 pp.   5 1/2 x 8 1/2 $6.95

Singles' Survival Guide

ISBN 1-55105-018-8   64 pp.   5 1/2 x 8 1/2 $6.95

Furniture Refinishing

ISBN 1-55105-022-6   64 pp.   5 1/2 x 8 1/2 $6.95

Look for these and other Lone Pine books at your local bookstore. If they're unavailable, order direct from:

Lone Pine Publishing
#206 10426-81 Avenue
Edmonton, Alberta   T6E 1X5
Phone: (403) 433-9333   Fax: (403) 433-9646